woodland
Creatures

CREATIVE NUDGINGS AND STEP-BY-STEP INSTRUCTIONS TO HELP YOU CREATE

• TIPS, TECHNIQUES, INSPIRATIONAL RAMBLINGS,

CHRISTI FRIESEN

Woods are wonderful. Tall trees, meandering vines, little furry creatures skittering through the underbrush. I grew up with a nice woods right behind my house and spent a lot of time running around among the trees. Ah, memories....

All that reminiscing about the woodlands got my creativity gears cranking, but led to a bit of a problem. Do you know how many possible woodland-themed projects I thought of, all of which could have been included in this book? A bajillion, that's how many!

But this book only has 48 pages, so I had to narrow down the choices.

Hopefully the ones I chose will amuse you.

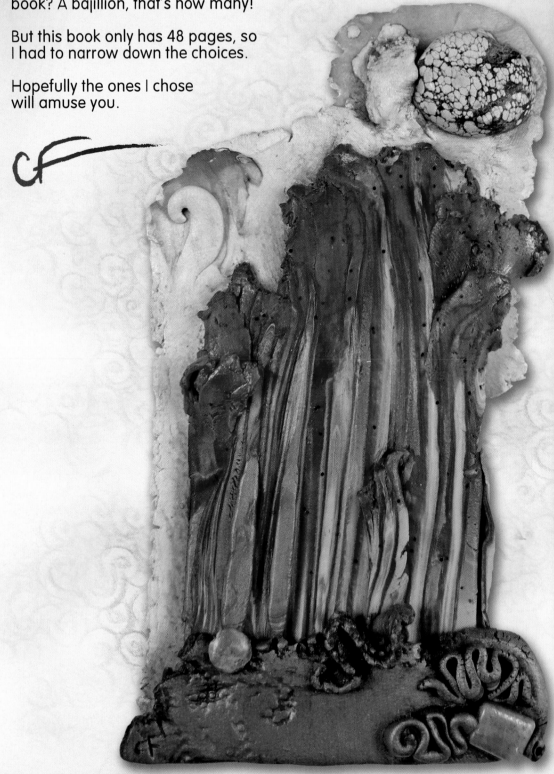

Polymer clay is pretty easy stuff to use. You're gonna' love it! (Unless you already do love it, in which case, you'll know a lot of the details I'm gonna talk about in the next few paragraphs, feel free to let your mind wander.)

Before using polymer, you'll need to condition it. Most of the time, you'll also want to mix special colors. There's a polymer clay overview in the very back of this book that goes over those basics. (Sneak back there whenever to read through it, if you need to. There'll be a quiz on it later.)

There are several brands of polymer clay, and all of them are groovy. I use and recommend Premo brand polymer clay for all the projects in this book, and for your further sculpting. Not too mushy, not too stiff…just right!

We'll also use liquid clay in these projects. I recommend Translucent Liquid Sculpey. It's a great item to have in your clay stash. It helps secure clay connections and it adheres new clay to baked clay.

There are several ways to add additional colors to polymer clay - baked and unbaked. One way is with mica powders, which add color and shine (and are absolutely addictive, hee hee). Mica powder goes on unbaked clay with a soft paintbrush, cotton swab or finger and bakes on permanently.

you can finish your piece with a clear satin glaze.

After clay is baked, acrylic paint can be added as a color addition as a light wash, or as accent color, or as a drybrush effect. My favorite way to use acrylic paint is to add it as patina, in an antiqueing effect. This is an optional step, as is adding a clear coating to protect and finish the clay. (Again, wander off into the back of the book for more details on adding a patina.)

One of the most fun things about polymer is how perfectly it combines with other media. A whole new level of creative possibilities open up when you begin to add embellishments and accents to your clay.

Embellishments

ribbon

silver leaf   paper

wool

head pins   lampwork glass eyes

beads

vintage & found objects

Whenever possible, embellishments are added to the clay with wire or headpins. How to do that will be explained as we go along. Why to do that is explained right now, at no extra charge: Beads and other accents won't stick in the clay permanently, and glue can be unreliable. Adding a wire anchor that embeds the accent into the clay is much more permanent. (Guess where those how-to details are?)

Wire can also be used as an embellishment, and it's invaluable as an armature (embedded in the clay to act as a support). We'll talk about all that stuff as we go along. Anything that can go into the oven along with the clay is perfect to use as an accent or embellishment – so that means all glass, crystal, stone, gems, natural pearls, metal, ceramic, feathers, fur and natural fibers. (Other stuff will work too - If you're not sure, just put a little bit of one of the accents in the oven at the usual temperature and see what happens. No melting, scorching or vaporizing? Use it!)

3

Oh, I noticed you noticed that I said "usual temperature" and you're wondering what that is, right? No? Oh. Well, anyway, that information is in the back of the book, too, along with all the other baking information. It's important stuff, so make sure to read up! Baking is the most important part of creating with polymer clay! (Luckily it's also the easiest if you follow a few guidelines.)

Tools are something every artist needs... and wants! We don't have to spend a lot of money on tools (but we still do, don't we). There are a few tools that are used the most often when working with polymer, and you'll want to have them for all the projects in this book. Additionally, there are a few tools that I've had specially created because I find them really, really useful. I think you might like them too. I refer to them in the projects in this book (by their initials) because they work just right. (Check in the 'Resources' section at the back of the book for more info on tools.) You don't have to rush right out and spend money on my tools (or any other tools), you can substitute anything you have lying around that is similar and it will work. (For example, no cutting blade? Use a sharp kitchen knife. No needle tool? Stick a needle or pin end into a log of clay, bake it – tah dah! homemade needle tool) Having the right tool can often make creating easier and more fun, but it's amazing what a little ingenuity can do when you need to stick to a tight budget!

great tools:
1. pliers & wire cutters
2. cutting blade
3. needle-nose tweezers
4. needle tool
5. craft knife

That's every-thing you need to know, so let's get claying!

pretty good tools:
1. paintbrush handle
2. plastic utensils
3. old dental tools
(make sure you rinse off the spit - eww.)
4. sharpened dowel

not-so-good tools:
1. pressed butterfly
2. rubber band
3. curly fry
4. chocolate (note: this is a good tool, however, for keeping up your creative energy!)

my favorite sculpting tools:
1. GHI = the "Gotta Have It" tool
2. WIA = the "Wow, It's Awesome" tool
3. CLWI – the "Can't Live Without It" tool

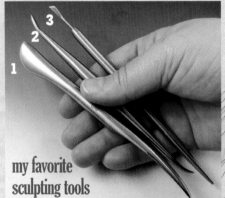

my favorite sculpting tools

Oh, by the way, stamps, texture sheets, and molds are wonderful things to use with polymer clay projects... you'll see!

When you have woodland creatures, you need woodlands. To have woodlands, you need woods. So, to get us in the mood for the creature projects, let's start with a woodsy project.

For this woodsy project, I picked the tree I like the best the oak. Apparently other artists like it too, because oak leaves and acorns have figured in decorative pieces for centuries. Oaks have interesting-looking leaves, and acorns are uniquely-shaped little weird nut-kinda' thingies (that's the scientific term for them, by the way). Together, leaf and acorn make a wonderful image combo!

NOTE: You don't have to make a brooch! Your Oak & Acorn creation can be a wall piece or an accent for an art quilt or whatever!

special stuff you'll need

- 8 decorative-tipped headpins
- 3 oval, green-colored pearls
- 2 vintage (or reproduction) filigree pieces
- mica powders: Antique Bronze, Spring Green
- pin back with locking bar – about 1.5"

Let's begin by making the oak leaf. Flatten a bit of the green clay mix in your hands, then run it through a pasta machine set to the widest setting. Take a tool with a pointy tip (I'm using my "WIA" tool) and embed a line in this sheet of clay – this will be the centerline of the leaf. Now press in the veins – lines going out from the centerline on each side.

clay colors
pale green =

2 green + 2 gold + 1 ecru pearl

light blue =

2 white + 1 (any) blue

Use a craft knife to cut the outline of the leaf. Start at the top and just cut a bump-out around each vein until you get to the bottom. Now cut a parallel line beside the center vein impression.

As we go along, I'll give you guides to make the clay blends. The numbers are proportions - for example, 2 parts gold + 1 part ecru = pale green. Got it?

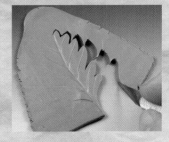

5

Knife back to the top of the leaf and cut out the other side in the same way.

This a rather free-form way to cut out the leaf, which amuses me, but if you prefer a bit more control, use a leaf pattern (there's one right over there in the margin, or you can create your own). Copy it onto paper, cut it out with scissors, use a needle tool to trace the outline onto the clay sheet and then cut it out with your craft knife. Now use the pointed tool to press the centerline and veins into the clay. That works nicely, doesn't it?

Let's soften that 'cookie cutter' look. Use a tool to press in between the lobes of the clay leaf. Use your fingers to press and gently pinch all along the outsides. This will take the sharpness off all the cut edges.

With your fingers, gently press the stem part all around and make the whole piece look rounded. You can push the bottom of the stem up gently to thicken it, if you want to.

Let's keep adding touches to increase the realism of the leaf. (Well, it's not going to be super-realistic, it's a stylized leaf, but we don't want it looking dorky.) Use a tool to press an indentation into the surface of the outer end of each lobe of the leaf. (I used my GHI tool cuz it's just the right shape – any tool with a rounded end should work.)

Press these dimples into each lobe. Now pick up the leaf and use your thumb and forefinger to gently press down in each indentation. This softens away the tool marks. Doesn't that look nifty? Unless of course you have long fingernails and you've left little nicks all over the leaf. Hmmm, go trim them and come back, I'll wait for you.

Of course this may press away the tips of all the veins, so use your pointy tool and re-make them as needed.

Oooh, goody, now it's powder time! Powder time is fun! I use mica powder (hence "powder time") to add color and shine to the clay. Refer back to the supplies page for tips on using mica powders if you skipped over that part.

CLEVER
THOUGHT
ALERT)

"The creation of a thousand forests is in one acorn.."
~ RALPH WALDO EMERSON

6

I chose an antique bronze-colored powder for the stem because it's a brown, but also added a bit of metallic, which will go with the metal accents we'll be adding soon (just in case you were wondering). Use a soft, small brush to dust the stem of the leaf with the powder and continue up the centerline. I also used a little green powder on the lobes of the leaf to make them glow. Doesn't that look great?

Ok, now make another leaf the same way, but a little smaller. (I didn't create a pattern for a smaller leaf, but you can just take the first leaf pattern and cut off a little of the paper all around to make it smaller.)

Once the smaller leaf is done, set both leaves aside and let's make an acorn. This is easy. Take some of the same green clay and roll out a little ball. Roll the ball into an oval. Use your fingers to pinchy-pinch the tip into a tiny point. (I pull a little, then turn the clay and pull more, then turn and start pinching and turning and pinching. This makes a nice even point.)

To make the cap and stem, just use a little bit of green clay and roll out another, smaller oval – about a third the size of the one we made the acorn from. Press this flat with your fingers and wrap it around the top of the acorn (the not-pointy end).

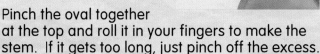

Pinch the oval together at the top and roll it in your fingers to make the stem. If it gets too long, just pinch off the excess.

Use a tool tip to press indentations into the cap. (I used the CLWI tool – boy, we've used all of my favorite tools in this project – see why they are my favorites!) Keep pressing all around and up to the stem. Press a few long lines into the stem if you want to. I did. A few notches pressed into the bottom of the cap complete that acorny look.

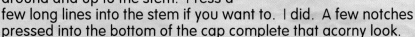

Use a bit of the bronze powder on the cap and the top half of the acorn to make the acorn more brown. This is a still-on-the-tree acorn, that's why it's mostly green. Of course you could have made the acorn out of brown clay, but that wouldn't have been as artsy-cool as this one.

To arrange the leaves and acorn into a nifty pattern, I chose to mix a light blue clay, roll it out into a sheet (turn the knob on your pasta machine a notch or two tighter to make a thinner sheet of clay), and then arrange the leaves and acorn on the blue clay. Make the grouping interesting. You can make more leaves and acorns if you want to.

Use your craft knife to cut all around the leaves/acorn, leaving a thin border. Soften the edges with your fingers.

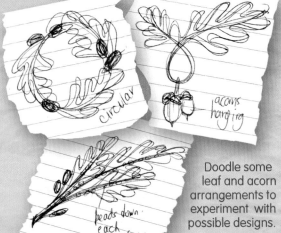

Doodle some leaf and acorn arrangements to experiment with possible designs.

Embellishment time! (This is even more

fun than powder time.) I was feeling a bit "Olde Timey" with this project, so when it came to adding the embellishments, I went with vintage metal findings and not a disco ball or something.

When adding beads and other accents, we have to make sure they will stay in the clay after it's baked. If you just press bits in, they will grab nicely to the sticky clay, but once the clay is baked and hardened, not so much. So, we have to use tricks to anchor in the accent pieces.

I wanted to add a curving accent to the top side of the brooch, so I used a circular vintage piece. You can use anything fun you have lying around (see the back of the book for some sources of fun stuff). Place the piece where you like it (I slipped it behind the clay so it would peek out) and then use a flattened piece of clay on the backside to sandwich the metal into place. Place the clay on the back and press lightly, then turn the piece over and set it down on your work-space to press more firmly from the front. This will help press the clays together around the metal, but allows you to see what you're doing so you don't smash the front details. Since the piece is a closed circle, it is anchored inside the clay and secure.

Now let's add a filigree bit to the center of one of the leaves. Use whatever looks nice. This piece had holes for attaching at top and bottom, which is convenient – just slip a headpin through each hole, trim off the excess wire with wire-cutters, leaving about an eighth of an inch or so, and then use pliers to bend a little hook in the end (like a fish hook shape).

Position the metal piece and press the headpins into the clay to secure it. If the pins are too long, they'll poke out the backside. You can patch that with a little flattened ball of clay to cover them, or add small balls of clay to the piece first and press the pins in on top of them.

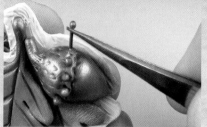

Next I used some decorative-tipped headpins (these are copper ball-tipped ones) to fancy up the rim of the acorn cap. Trim and bend a tight hook in the ends. Push them far enough so that the decorative tips embed into the clay just a little.

How about a little color?
Maybe some nice, green pearls? Yeah!

The pearls need to be wired on. This is a little trick that you will use every time you want to add beads to your clay. Since it's one of those things you'll use all the time, I've added that how-to sequence to the back of the book for handy reference. Quick, zip back there right now and read it!

Good, you're back. So wire up some pearls and press them into the tips of one of the leaves. (Since I used end-drilled pearls, I had to lay my pearls down with the hooks imbedded, but with much of the wire still exposed. Don't worry, I have a plan.)

Whenever possible, I hide exposed wire with clay that looks like it's just part of the design. In this case, small dots and ovals of clay cover the wire and add to the decorative look of the piece. A touch of powders finishes it nicely, don't you think?

Look your creation all over – does it need anything? Any extra fancy-bits? How about a little more bronze mica powder to make the bottom leaf look more shaded? Ahhh, perfect.

Time to bake the piece. Then we'll add whatever backing you've chosen – pin or wall hanging hook.

Baking is an essential step to the clay process. It's easy, but important that you get it correct so that your piece is strong. I've tucked that info in the back of the book too, so we don't take up space in every project with those details. So zip back there now and read about baking.

Bake your piece. Let it cool.

To add a pin back to make this into a brooch, or a hook back to make it into a wall piece, I think it's best to add the hardware after all the sculpting is done and firmly saved by baking. The information on how to add either is… you guessed it!… in the back of the book!

Now add a patina with brown acrylic, if you want to. I wanted to. (Information about adding patina is also in the back of the book.)

Don't leaf this pin lying around – wear it and get all those well-deserved ooohs and aaaahs.

My! aren't YOU a handsome fellow!

When you think of woodland creatures, you think of squirrels, right? Hmm, well I do, and the three people I asked did too, so I think that's pretty solid research. Anyway, squirrels are fun to sculpt, so let's make one.

special stuff you'll need

- one 4mm or 6mm dark, round bead (eye)
- eight small pearls, grey color (or similar beads)
- natural wool, grey (see back of book for sources)

Not all squirrels are grey of course, but it is a pretty common color, so start by making the grey clay blend. With this clay, roll a ball about the size of a small hard-boiled egg yolk. This will be the body (we'll add the head and tail later).

clay colors
grey =

2 silver + 1 burnt umber + 1 white

Squirrels do this sorta' hunching thing that makes their backsides bump out. To get that shape, first squeeze/roll one side of the ball into a cone shape.

white =

1 white (DUH!)

The cone-shaped end will become the curve of his back and neck area, and the rounded end his rump. I know that sounds kinda' vague, but trust me. (pssst... it's not always a good idea to trust anyone who says "trust me", but in this case you can trust me, honest).

This squirrel project is great as a focal bead! — When you string it up into a necklace, wouldn't it look cool to add some little leaf beads and maybe some acorn dangles?

Keep pinching to make that cone into a thinner, more-pointy cone. Use your fingers to curve the narrow end upwards. Now it looks like a comma, lying down. Use your cutting blade to slice off the tip of the cone.

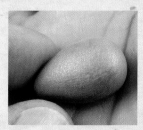

Obviously, now we have to make a head. Well, we don't have to, we could create a headless squirrel, but frankly, that's kind of creepy. So, for the head just roll out a small ball of clay (about the size of a large olive) and then pinch/roll it to make it more egg-shaped.

Use your blade to snicker-snack off a slice where the head will connect to the neck slice. Connect them!

Press firmly (but no smooshing!) and use a tool to blend the clays together at the connection. If he looks like a mutant peanut so far, you've done it correctly.

Let's add the eye. Wire up a dark, round bead (like a garnet or black onyx) in the usual way (the back of the book has that info if you need a refresher). Before we press it in, let's add some white clay around the eye – lots of squirrels have white fur around their eyes. It's a fashion statement. Roll out a small ball of white clay and press it onto the center of the face. Press hard enough to flatten it.

Remember that the ball will get larger as it flattens (obviously), so don't make the ball too big or he'll no longer be fashionable, he'll be a doofus. Now use the tip of a tool to press a hole in the center of this white clay blob.

Press the eye bead into the hole – push the bead so that only half the bead is left exposed.
      Ahhhhh, so cute already!

While you've got the white clay out, let's add some white fur coloring to his chest (also very fashionable this season). Roll out a little ball of white clay and then press it reeeeeeally flat with your fingers to make a piece that will cover him from chin to belly (but not so much that it spreads out to his sides). Press it on firmly.

We can't just leave the clay wad on the chest, that would be silly. Use a tool to firmly stroke the edges of the white clay onto the grey clay (use the edge of the WIA tool for this). This creates a furry edge to the white clay, which looks more natural. Do the same to the white around the eye – drag it gently with your tool to make it blend into the grey clay.

BoiNK

It's all fun & games until somebody gets hurt – but ooooh! what fun until then!

11

Now the part you've been waiting for – the tail! Without a big, fluffy tail, the squirrel is just a dull, little mousy thing, but with the tail, he's faaaaabulous! Take about as much clay as you did for the body and roll it into a fat log. Taper one end of the log into a blunt point. Curl that point around your finger to make a "J" shape. Taper the other side just a little. Bend it the other way to make the "J" into an "S".

Press the "J" end of the tail firmly onto the squirrel body in the tail-attachment area (or 'butt' as it's sometimes referred to). Use a tool to blend the clays together.

We'll come back to the tail soon, but now let's give his face some more squirrelly features!

To make a nose, just roll out a little ball of grey clay and place it on the tip of his snout.

Press down to flatten the upper end only of the nose ball (the end towards the forehead).

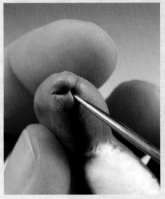

Use a tool to blend the flattened clay onto the face smoothly.

For the mouth, first press a line straight down below the center of the nose. A needle tool works well for this part.

Now press curved lines going out from each end of that line to create the mouth. Sorta' a roundy "W" kind of thing.

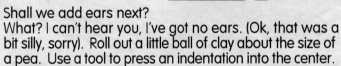

If the curve is visible on the front side of the face, you've done it right! Doesn't he look like a happy squirrel now?

Shall we add ears next?
What? I can't hear you, I've got no ears. (Ok, that was a bit silly, sorry). Roll out a little ball of clay about the size of a pea. Use a tool to press an indentation into the center.

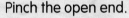
Pinch the open end.

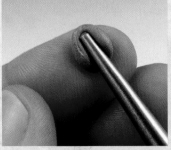

It's easier to add this ear if we slice off a little of the excess blobbage that was created by pinching the end. Just use a cutting blade and cut at a slight angle.

Press the cut part of the ear onto the face in the ear area (behind the eye but in front of the neck and up towards the top of the head). Use a tool to blend the end of the ear into the head clay.

Make another ear in the same way and press it on the back of the head. (Remember that the indentation side points towards the back. Hey! You can just press an ear shape if you want instead of bothering with the indention part – nobody will know).

Ok, face looking good! On to the lil' feets and arms. Let's start with the arms. Roll out two little balls of clay about the size of almonds. Roll each into a log with one end slightly tapered.

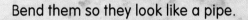

Bend them so they look like a pipe.

On each "pipe" arm, use a little blade to cut two equally-spaced-apart slices. Make the cut on the thinner end. (I suggest using the tip of the CLWI tool – it works great.)

Tah dah! Arms with lil' squirrelly fingers.

Use your cutting blade again to slice off a little of the excess at the top of the arms (in the armpit area ... do squirrels have armpits?) and press the arms onto the clay body in the shoulder area (below the neck, above the belly.)

One on the front and one on the back. Press the cut side onto the body, obviously.

A squirrel's back leg has a pretty pronounced haunch (or is it a thigh? Knee? I really can't remember the exact body part name... if only I had paid more attention in my rodent anatomy class!) Anyway, roll out a ball of clay about the size of an m&m (plain, not peanut) and flatten it slightly.

Press it into place on the only spot left for a haunch/thigh/ knee and use a tool to blend only the side nearest the tail into the body - this will leave the front of the flattened circle unblended.

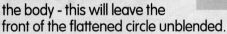

To add the foot and toes, first roll out a log of clay and then use your blade to slice one end off at an angle.

For the back leg, you can skip the flattened circle part, and just press on another leg log. Cut two lines into the front of each to create the toes (same way as we did on the fingers).

So now your squirrel should look pretty good – a little naked, but good! Adjust the arms and legs so that everything is visible and balanced.

Time to add furry-ness! This will be a two-step process – fur texture, and added fibers. To add the fur texture, use short strokes with a tool tip (try the flatter end of the WIA tool). Remember to follow the lines that fur would actually grow. If you don't know how squirrel fur grows, lure one to your work station with peanuts. Or "google images" works well too. Add fur strokes to the whole surface <u>except</u> for the cheeks, nose, hands and feet. Include strokes on the tail, even though we're going to add fibers there.

As you already know, one of the most fantastic things about polymer clay is how wonderfully it accommodates other media, like fiber! (Which we're going to use next to make the tail super fluffy!)

I chose natural raw wool (like the kind used in felting) but any natural fiber will work well. Many yarns, even if they are synthetic or blends will also work. To test, just snip a bit off the skein, put it on a piece of foil and pop it in the oven to see how it holds up in the heat – if it doesn't melt, use it!

We're going to add just a little bit of wool at a time to slowly build up the fluffiness. Pull a small bit of fibers from the clump. Twirl one end in between your fingertips to make a compact end (a bit of moisture on your fingertips helps).

To add the little clump of fiber, first poke a hole in the tail clay (start at the tip and then we'll work our way down, it's easier that way). Add a drop of liquid clay to the hole (this will 'grab' the fibers and help secure them to the clay).

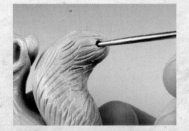

Press the fibers (compact side first) into the hole.
It really helps to use needle-nose tweezers for this.

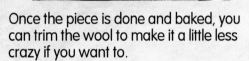

After the fiber is pressed firmly into the hole, use a
tool to smooth the clay up to the fiber clump to
keep everything tight.

Keep on going – poke a hole, liquid clay,
clump of fiber, smooth with tool, until the
whole tail is nice and fluffy.

Once the piece is done and baked, you
can trim the wool to make it a little less
crazy if you want to.

Well, you can stop right there if you'd like,
but why? Let's fancy this dude up a little. I
love adding beads and little curls of clay,
it adds a nice dollop of art-fullness.

I think some deep grey pearls will look
groovy, but you can use anything you like. We can add the beads one at a time, but
we can also add a little line-up of beads too. Use wire cutters to snip off a couple
inches of 28 gauge wire. Use pliers to bend a hook in one end. Slide on three
pearls (or other beads). Trim off the excess wire to leave just about a quarter
of an inch on each side of the bead lineup.
Bend a hook in the other end too.

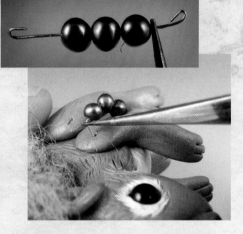

Use needle nose tweezers to press the
bead lineup into the clay. Press the wire
in on one side, then on the other.
I added this to the squirrel's upper arm.

Now make another bead lineup – 5 pearls
this time – and add it to the upper leg.
Follow the curves of the clay.

You can add little balls of clay to cover any
wire that is still visible.

Make a little curl of clay to tuck in
under the leg pearls,
if there is room.
It just looks
fun, I think.

*Nifty,
huh?*

15

Finally, a bit of mica powder will add some touches of color. A little russet on the nose and inner ear and finger/toe tips looks especially nice.

Now it's time to add a hole so that you can string this cutie into a necklace later. Use a needle tool to carefully pierce a hole through his upper chest and on through the tail. I usually press a thick piece (16 gauge) of straight, uncoated wire through this hole to keep it nice and straight while the piece is baking. Afterwards, use pliers to twist and then pull it out.

Oh, by the way, I added a little tuft of fiber to his head. He needed a hairdo.

Bake the finished piece (don't worry, the wool and pearls will be fine!) for the usual time and temperature (the back of the book has that info if you need it).

Once the clay is cool, use dark brown acrylic paint to add a patina (again, check the back of the book for a refresher if you need it). Don't get the paint in the tail fuzz! You can add a clear coating if you want to, but it doesn't really need it.

Ooh! What a cute little scampery chipmunk!

it's easy to use the same steps that we just used to make the squirrel in order to make a chipmunk. The ears are a little smaller, and the tail is pointy and upturned, instead of a fluff wad. Add the characteristic chipmunk stripes by pressing on thin snakes of black and white clays.

Oh, and a lil' pink nose of course!

16

As I may have mentioned, there are so many more woodland creaturey projects I could have added to this book, but there's just not eough room ... sigh. But good news! I have lots of room on my website! So, if you still want to make more woodland creatures by the time you get to the end of this book, here's some other projects to play with!

"Luna Moth"

I don't know if luna moths hang out in the woods, but I think so. I grew up with forests all around my house and we had luna moths in the summer, but of course they always seemed to be lounging around the porch light.
Silly lounge moths.

"Cute Critter"

I'm not sure what kind of rodent this is … he has a mousey face, but his tail is too fluffy. Pikas have fluffy tails, but they're more round all over. He really looks like a Loatian Rock Rat, but they're grey…. oh well, who cares! He's a critter, and he's cute and he lives in the woods, that's good enough.

Besides download-able projects, check out my online classes -- sooooo fun!

"Here's Looking At You"

This is a wall mirror project and look at how woodsy it is! Pine trees! Ooh! And a blue jay kinda' bird. Doesn't that look fun to make? (pssst: it is!)

go to "downloadable projects" at
www.CForiginals.com

17

Lots of woodland creatures live in hollow trees, or so I've learned from Saturday morning cartoons. The nifty thing about this project is that the "hollow tree" is also a vessel that can hold water, so you can slip in a few actual leafy tree branches inside, which adds an unexpected bit of realism.

As usual, let's start by conditioning clay and mixing colors. The colors for the raccoon are to be thoroughly blended, so mix them first.

The tree blend is more interesting to create. First gather up your clay. The proportions don't need to be exact. I gathered the tree-colored scraps around my work area (stay away from the purple clay, unless you're doing a Dr. Seuss-style tree).

special stuff you'll need
- mica powder: brown
- two 4mm dark, round beads (eyes)
- toilet paper
- 20 gauge wire: two inches

Smash the clays up into a nice, big wad. Flatten it with your hands or a roller and run the whole mess through the pasta machine on the widest setting. Fold the sheet and run it through again. Now adjust the pasta machine to tighten the rollers two or three notches. Run the clay through one more time and hold your hand under the rollers to catch the clay as it comes through. This should make the sheet pleat back and forth.

Use a cutting blade to slice the pleat into thick slices (about a quarter of an inch thick, or maybe just a little less). Press these slices together, side-to-side, exposing the sliced sections.

Press firmly to connect them.

clay colors
tree blend =
gold + burnt umber + ecru + black

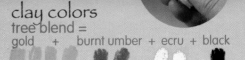

tree inside =
gold

black fur =
black

cream fur =
white + gold

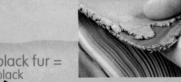

dark brown fur =
black + burnt umber

grey-brown fur =
silver + burnt umber + white

Now flatten the resulting slice of clay a little (with fingers or roller) so that you can run the whole thing through the pasta machine. Wait! First set those rollers back to the widest setting again! Fold the sheet and run it through again. Repeat several times, making sure that you look at it on both sides each time so that you can fold it with the most interesting blends facing out each time.

What we're trying to accomplish is a sheet of clay with a marbled, striped pattern that isn't so bold that it looks like it escaped from the circus, but not so subtle that it just looks like a smear of peanut butter. Once you have it looking nice, stop folding! Just tighten the pasta machine rollers a few notches and run the sheet through once, just to thin it.

During this whole process, don't slice the edges to make them straight! You'll want rough, crackly edges if possible! You can rip and re-position the clay to keep the sheet rectangular, but no cutting. This means you, over there – I see you! Put down that cutting blade!

Set aside the stripey blend, and run some gold clay through the machine until you have a sheet about the same size and thickness as the stripey one.

Lay the gold sheet down, place the stripey sheet on top (prettiest side up) and press down gently to connect them together into one sheet. This double sheet will become the tree. In order to make the tree hollow, but give it something firm to form around and hold its shape during sculpting, we need a material that is durable but easily removable. Guess what works great? Pudding! No, not pudding. That's silly. And messy. What works really great is toilet paper! Not kidding! It does!

Go get a wad of tp and roll it up into a cylindrical glob. Get it wet and squeeze it to wring out the drips. Add damp tp as needed to build up the shape until you have a hollow-tree-sized clump. It's a good idea to finish it by wrapping some dry tp around it to keep all the bits together, then squeeze it.

Set down the damp tp, and pick up the tree-color clay sheet in your hands. Hold it for a while to warm up the clay.

Place the tp wad in the center of the clay sheet (gold-side up) and wrap the clay up and around it, like a candy wrapper. Take your time and manipulate the clay so that all the wrinkles are spaced in a somewhat even manner. Oh, and leave the top open! This part takes a little patience, you have to help the folds and wrinkles look tree-bark-ish.

At this point it helps to press the whole thing down onto your work surface, to flatten the bottom. Then you can use your fingers more easily to pinch the clay into position all around. 19

Once you have the whole piece pinched together, cradle the whole thing in your hands, with the opening facing you. Use a tool with a flat surface (the narrow end of the GHI tool works great) and drag it towards you to smooth the clay and minimize the depth of the creases. This part takes patience too - smooth a little at a time, all around the tree, smoothing, shaping, blending.

Use a smaller-tipped tool to refine the blends and add bark-like texture (try the wider end of the WIA tool for this part).

You're finished with this part when it looks like a tree trunk.

To make the hole, first find the part of your tree you'd like to be the front. Next use a cutting blade or craft knife to slice two intersecting lines like a 'plus' sign about halfway up the tree.

Tuck each section of the slices up inside the tree. Just push, the tp will move out of the way. Hold your fingers on the outside of the tree and press the flap with a finger from the inside to join the flap to the inside of the tree. Clean up any cut edges with the tool again. Oh, by the way, if there are some rough and crackly areas, that's good! It adds a nice tree-ish texture.

Don't you think a tree knot would add a nice touch? Me too. Make a thick snake from some of the tree clay blend, if you still have some bit lying around. Roll it up into a messy curl.

Press it onto the tree and use a tool to blend in the edges

so it looks like it grew there. You can add another snake of clay beside it for extra interest. Blend that in too.

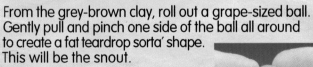

And we're all done with the tree. Bake it for 30 minutes in a preheated oven to firm it up (back of the book has baking details, you remember).While that's baking and then cooling, let's make a raccoon! We'll make a head, arms and a tail – the rest of him will be hidden in the tree (how convenient!)

From the grey-brown clay, roll out a grape-sized ball. Gently pull and pinch one side of the ball all around to create a fat teardrop sorta' shape. This will be the snout.

Use your fingers to push down on the cone while holding the bottom of the cone at a slight upturned angle, to create a forehead. This is easier than it sounds, honest.

To make the indentations for his eyes, aim the snout forward and press gently with your thumbs above and on either side of the snout.

Make the head a little more pointy – just press down on the top of the eye socket area a little tiny bit.

To make the ears, first roll out little teardrops of clay, then use a tool to press an indentation in the centers (again the WIA tool is perfect for this!). With a blade, slice off the extra blobby bits at the bottom of the ears.

Press the sliced ends of each ear onto the head - on the top and slightly to the sides. Placement is important – too close together on top and it's a kitty, too far apart on the sides and it's a … um… awkward-looking creature of some sort. Use a tool to carefully blend the ears into the head. If the ear tips are too pointy, round them out a bit with a tool tip and finger.

Ok, now, if you've looked at any raccoons lately, you'll have noticed all the interesting contrasts of color – light snout, and of course those dark "bandit" eyes, even so lighter color fur above the dark eye fur… rather stylish, actually. Let's start with the snout. Take a bit of that cream-colored clay mix, roll out a tiny ball and flatten it very flat with your fingers. Wrap it around the snout. Press it on firmly, but gently.

For the bandit eyes, roll out two tiny balls from the dark brown color blend, flatten them and press them into the eye socket area.

Raccoons have a little band of light-colored fur above the dark eye fur. Roll out tiny snakes of the cream-colored clay and press them on over the brown circles.

Now the fun part! Let's make these patches of color look like fur. Use the pointy tip of a tool to gently drag the edges of these added clay bits onto the clay of the face. Short, light strokes do the trick. It will take several strokes to get the clay to blend so don't rush it. Oh, and be sure to hold the head with a very light grip or else you'll squish it. Blend in a natural way, too – the snout color goes straight back onto the cheeks and forehead. The eye color blends away from the center of the face like a comet's tail.

Add eyes! Dark beads work the best. Wire them up in the usual way (back of the book for info if you need it) and press them into the center of the dark eye patches.

A nose is just a little oval of black clay pressed onto the tip of the snout.

21

Isn't he cute already? Now gently set the head aside.

He needs at least one arm to hang out of the tree hole. Maybe two. Not three, that would be weird.

Arms start as a log of clay, just like the squirrel arm. Hmmm, as a matter of fact, just repeat the steps from the squirrel project to create the fingers. (How about three slices this time to make four fingers (of course raccoons have five fingers, but we can fudge a little). Separate the fingers a little and use a tool to smooth in between them. Pinch the tips of each finger into a bit of a point (sort of a 'claw' kinda look).

Probably you'll need to narrow the wrist and arm a bit, just pinch a roll.

If you want, you can dust the tips of each claw with a little brownish mica powder.

Perfect. If you want, you can make another arm and hand. You'll probably need it. Or wait to see if you need it later, and then make it.

The tail is fun to make. First create one more because the cream-colored mix is too light, and the body blend is too dark, so mix equal parts of each together for the just-right color – let's just call it tan color.

Roll out two tail shapes (yup, two... you'll see why). One from the new tan color and one from the dark brown clay. By the way, a 'tail shape' is just a thick log with tapered ends – sorta' like a big grain of rice.

Place them both side-by-side, and with a blade cut both of them about an eighth of an inch from the tip.

Take the tan clay tip and press it onto the brown tail.

Lay them together again and cut again – a thinner slice this time.

Press the tan tip & brown ring section onto what's left of the tail.

Get the idea? Good! Keep going until you have a completely striped tail.

Gently press all over to connect and smooth the sections. Now use your tool tip to make it furry – you know how! Just drag gentle strokes all over.

Ok, that's all the raccoon bits, so let's assemble the whole thing!

First retrieve the baked hollow tree part. There's toilet paper in it! Who put that in there… oh yeah…. To get it out, bring it to the sink and turn the water on it to re-soak the tp. Use pliers or tweezers to yank out clumps of wet tp until the tree is hollowed out. Dry it off.

Since the unbaked raccoon bits won't stick well to the baked clay of the tree, we'll use liquid clay to make it all work out. Start with an arm. Add a little liquid clay to the underside.

Press the upper arm onto the inside of the tree and press firmly with your fingertip to connect it. Next, bend the arm through the hole and press it down onto the outside of the trunk. Liquid clay should be at the connection points, add more if you need it.

Squeeze a little liquid clay onto the underside of the tail and press it into place – I chose to place mine on the opposite side of the hole from the arm and to make it point up.

Now we need to make a body blob for inside the trunk. This will serve two purposes – it will give the illusion of a whole raccoon's-worth of creature inside, and it will give the head something to attach to.

It's tricky to place the body in the trunk since the trunk is narrow, so I added the liquid clay to the side that will attach, then poked a needle tool in the top of the clay blob to hold onto while I lowered the clay inside. If you angle the tree onto its side with the hole/raccoon bits aimed down, gravity will help keep the blob in place while you get a finger in there to press the blob firmly to the inside of the tree. Be careful not to smoosh the arm and tail!

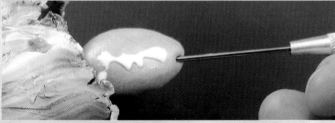

Once the body blob is firmly in place, we can add the head. For extra support, snip an inch of 20 gauge wire and bend it in half. Slip the ends of the wire into the body blob and leave the bend showing. Add a drop or two of liquid clay onto the clay, around the wire.

Hold the head up to the wire – how's it look? Do you need another arm to make the whole assembly look right? If so, make one and attach it, if not, on to the next step!

Press the head onto the wire and firmly connect to the body. I tilted it on an angle for maximum cuteness. Be careful not to smoosh it!

Now that the pieces are all in place, use the edge of your tool to add strokes of fur texture all over (except on the fingers and the nose). Doesn't that make it look good!

little
stroke of brown mica powder right down the center of his head from the base of the nose to the forehead – a very raccoony detail.

You're done!

Time to bake the whole thing again! Insert another wad of tp into the trunk to help wedge the body blob firmly in place while it bakes (no need to get it wet this time). Bake at the usual temperature for a full 45 minutes to an hour. Let it cool completely. Add a dark brown acrylic paint patina to the tree to bring out the details.

Whatcha' think? **Nifty, right?!**

You can get a little fancy by adding the rest of the body, then tucking the racoon into the branches of a full sculptural tree. This takes a little more work of course, and there's no toilet paper involved, alas. I'll show you how to do this project one of these days....

A faerie fox?

Flying? What?

It's a folklore thing. The flying Faerie Foxes are mystic spirits in the tales of the Kitsune Forest - nomadic tribes. The elders told of these tiny airborne creatures who lured travelers deep into the woods so they could trick them into giving up all their sandwiches and cookies. Hee hee... sounded convincing for a minute, huh?

Actually, I just thought a flying faerie fox would be fun to make. I don't know why, it's just how my brain works, apparently. If you prefer, your fox doesn't have to be a faerie, and it doesn't have to fly! It can just be an articulated fox figure. Of course, then you'll miss out on making the nifty wings.

special stuff you'll need

. two eyes: lampwork glass eyes, or round beads (4-6mm)

. two decorative headpins (ball-tipped preferably)

. fibrous paper (mulberry paper or similar): 2 pieces each 5" square

. colored pencils

. ribbon: about 20"

. sharp craft knife

. 20 gauge wire: about 8"

. acrylic paint: light brown, red-brown, dark brown

. craft glue, white, all-purpose.

Hard to believe this is polymer clay, isn't it? it really looks like carved wood!

clay

black

Sculpey "UltraLight"

Of course you can use a carving technique with any polymer clay, but this project uses Sculpey UltraLight. The UltraLight is special. It's a super-lightweight clay that's kinda' fluffy (it feels like marshmallow!). This makes carving the baked clay much much easier.

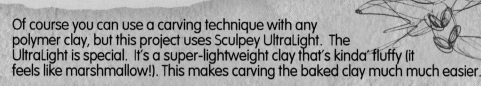

All the parts of this fox are made out of the UltraLight clay, which is only available in white – but don't worry! We'll be adding color after it's baked.

One thing you need to know before you start – UltraLight is very soft, so you probably don't need to condition it, just mash it a bit in your hands before you begin. Keep a light touch with this project! It smooshes easily, so hold the shapes gently. Don't forget that we will be carving the finished pieces, so lumps and blobby bits are no big deal, you'll have a chance to cut them to shape!

Ready? Begin! Roll a ball for the head, about the size of a small hard-boiled egg yolk.

Foxes have tufts of fur that stick out just a bit from their cheeks, and we're going to greatly exaggerate that, just because we can. So, gently pinch and pull a tapered point from one side of the clay ball to make one cheek tuft.

Do the same on the other side to match, so the shape looks like a ball that swallowed a banana.

Pull the snout out in the same way we did the raccoon snout. Pull out a knob, centered between the cheek tufts, on the front side of the ball.

The next part is kinda tricky – not hard to do, but you just have to have an idea in your head of what it is going to look like when it's done, in order to make it look like it's going to look like. That's not confusing at all, is it? So look at the picture again of the finished fox's face – see the tufts and the snout? Good, now look at the ears. See where they are? Now make them! Pull and pinch in the same way as we've been doing so far, just smaller and more pointy. The ears are on the top of the head, above the cheek tufts!

Once you've pulled an ear shape out, gently flatten it a little (the flat side faces the front).

Ok, so this is what it should look like so far - snout, ears, cheeky things… it's kinda' like a confused starfish at this stage.

Now we'll add the eyes – this will really make a difference – from spikey marshmallow blob to some sort of actual creature! I used two lampwork glass eyes (I've got an eye guy - see the 'resources' section in the back if you want some of these cool eyes, too). If you use a pair of glass eyes, just press them in, wire side first. Take your time to make sure the pupils line up –

they like to wander off in different directions, then the fox will look like he's off his meds. If you prefer, you can use two dark, round beads instead of glass eyes. Wire them up and press them in front and center.

If you like the way the eyes look, leave them just like that! Or you can add some eyebrows. Just roll a little bit of clay into a rice-shaped bit, curve it a little and press into place above (and just a little on top of) the eyeball/bead. Make one for each eye, and blend them into the face clay a little (use a tool, or your Jedi powers).

Press some indentations into the ear centers.

(My thanks to Sarah Shriver for the idea of carving UltraLight.)

To add a smile, use a needle tool to press (not scratch) a curved line into the front of the snout – not right in the center, more toward the bottom of the clay nob.

Now press in another line, from the mouth line straight up - just a short line - this separates the upper snout into cheeks.

He needs a nose. Roll out a little oval of black clay. Flatten it a little and cut it in half to make a half-circle shape. Soften the cut edge with your fingers and press it on the top of the snout, right above the short line.

Faeries need antenna, I don't know why, it's just a faerie thing, I guess. I used headpins with an enameled-ball tip. You can use the same, or any ball or decorative tipped pin. Trim the wire ends to the right length (don't forget that some of the wire will be inside the clay), bend a hook in the ends, and press them into the clay at the top of the head. Use a tool to smooth the clay around the wires if there are any gouges.

Next let's bake the head to prevent mushing when it gets attached to the body. First though, let's add a wire so that we can attach it to the body later! Bend a short piece of 20 gauge wire (about an inch) in half. Bend one end into a hook. Carefully insert the wire into the back of the head, where the neck would be. Remember how mushy the clay is and try to insert it without mashing anything on the front. Faerie foxes hate it when their faces mash.

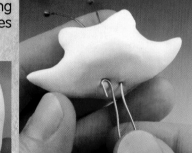

Preheat your oven, make a little nest of toilet paper, set the head in the tp nest to keep everything smush-free, and bake it for 20-30 minutes.

While the head is baking and then cooling, let's make the body blob. Just roll out an oval that is a little less than twice as big as the head. Set that aside.

Now let's make the tail. Start with a blob (about as big as the head blob - foxes have big tails, so it's ok). Form the blob into a log, then taper both ends to a blunt point.

We need to add a wire to the inside of the tail to add strength and to help it stay on, so snip another piece of 20 gauge wire. Make it just a little longer than the tail. Bend a

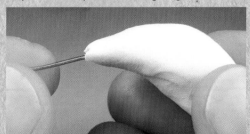

hook into one end. Curve the wire a little into a mildly-amused smile arch (not a maniacal grin). Press the not-hook end into the tail (curve the clay to follow the curve of the wire), and leave the hook end with about half an inch or so of wire sticking out.

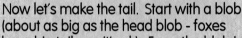

27

Press the hook end into the body to connect the tail. Use a tool to blend the tail clay to the body clay. (UltaLight blends weird compared to Premo, doesn't it? Just roll with it!). You can add a drop of liquid clay to make the pieces blend easier, if you want to.

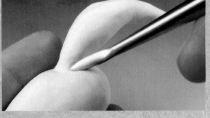

If you prefer your fox to be a sitting-down-on-the-shelf kinda' creature, press the tail into the body at a perpendicular angle so that he can sit down without the tail being in the way

Now we are going to add some channels so that we can attach the arms and legs after the pieces are all done and baked. Use a needle tool to poke a hole through the body at the hip level and another at the shoulder level. Push a piece of thick wire through the hole to keep it open.

Ok, the head should be done baking by now. Once it's cool, press the neck wire into the top of the body/tail blob. Oh wait! Add a little liquid clay to the connection point first to help the clays grip. Blend the clay of the body up onto the head using a tool, or your fingers.

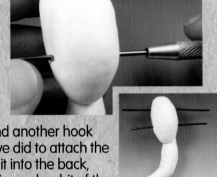

Now is the time to add a hook on the back so we can hang it up later. Bend another hook thingy (just like the one we did to attach the head to the body). Push it into the back, just below the neck, leaving only a bit of the hook exposed.

Great! On to the legs and arms – these are stinkin' easy!

The arms are just little logs with a bit of a bend to them. With a needle tool, pierce a hole through the top of each arm log. This will correspond to the hole through the body.

The back legs (which will be the ones at the bottom, since the fox will be sorta' standing up) are very similar to the ones we just made, so roll out two more logs – make them a little longer and maybe just a bit thicker. Make a bend in the leg a little lower than halfway down. Fox legs bend like dog legs – backwards compared to human legs.

Add a hole to the top of these legs too, corresponding to the hip hole. Now, all the bits are done! Bake all of them! The usual time and temperature.

Once everything is cool, it's carving time! Ok, a few words of safety-warning are appropriate right about now. In order to carve the baked clay best, you need to use a new craft knife, nice and sharp.

Hmmm, now what is it I was supposed to tell you about carving with sharp blades... oh yeah... when using a super sharp knife always cut towards your major arteries... wait, that doesn't seem right. Probably the opposite of that would be better.

Short, shallow, controlled strokes are best. Start with the arms, they're easiest to carve. The idea is to shave away the whole surface leaving those tell-tale little carve chunks behind, making everything look like carved wood.

Work over all the pieces as best you can. You probably won't be able to carve in the face area, but you can get the forehead and cheek tufts, and luckily, that's enough.

Pretty fun, huh? So, once the carving is all done, it's time to add the paint that will make it look like a fox and not a ghost.

This is different from the antique-style patina we've used so far on the other projects. This will be a wash of color, used as a surface treatment.

Start with a light brown acrylic paint and water it down so it's very thin and runny. Use a paintbrush to apply it over the whole surface of the fox. Pat off the excess with a sponge as you go along. The result should be just the hint of beige-ish color all over, a little darker possibly in the cracks and crevices.

Let's start with the head. Use a brush to paint the reddish paint on. It should still have a watercolory feel to it, so just add a very light coating.

Next we'll add the classic "red fox" color, also with acrylic paint. I used a burnt sienna (a nice red-brown tone) with a touch of red added to enrich the tint. Water this down a bit too, but not as much as the first paint.

The reddish color should go from the base of his black nose, up the facial bridge of the nose and over the top of this head and ears. Only the top halves of the cheek tufts should be painted. Blot gently with a sponge or with a bit of toilet paper (handy stuff, toilet paper, isn't it?)

Doesn't that look great?

Continue painting and blotting - all four legs can be painted entirely. The back of the head and all the back of the body get the red treatment.

Bring the tint onto the front and back of the tail, but leave a good portion of the tip unpainted.

Finally, let's add dark brown paint for the last details. Dab it on the ends of all the legs. Use a paintbrush to add a ring of dark brown above the blank tail tip. And of course darken the ear tips. Let it all dry.

Time to assemble! We'll use ribbons to attach the legs and arms to the body. This makes them moveable, which is rather cute. Hey, I know a sneaky way to get the ribbon in those little holes. Take a piece of 28 gauge wire (about 6 inches) and bend it in half. Stick the bent end through the hole (let's start with the hip hole). Now slip the ribbon through the wire bend and pull the wire/ribbon through the hole, pulling the ribbon with it. Then pull the ribbon out of the wire.

Holes too small? Use a hand-held drill to enlarge them.

Now insert the bent wire into one leg (the bend should poke towards the body). Slip in the end of the ribbon sticking out of the hip hole and pull it and the wire through the leg.

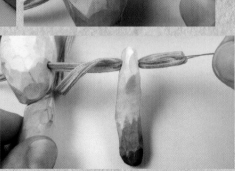

Tie a knot in the end and pull it tight to bring the leg firmly against the body.

Continue the same process to attach the other leg to the other side. Pull the ribbon tight, and tie the knot firmly.

Tie the arms on in the same way.

Time for wings. Start by cutting your fibrous papers into two half-circles about 5 inches wide. Now use colored pencils to add some fun color – I suggest keeping most of the color on the outer edges of the circles. Pencil both sides of the paper.

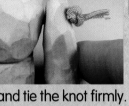 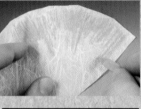 

Draw lines, curls, whatever looks fun Pick colors that complement the ribbon/eyes/antenna….

Now for a little simple origami. Fold the circle in half.

And in half again. And again. And again – until you have a small wedge. Now snip, snip a little "v" in the center with sharp scissors.

Open it back up – foldy and jaggedy!

Snip a piece of 20 gauge wire, oh about 4 or 5 inches should do it. Feed it through the hook on the back of the fox. Wrap it around a few times and use pliers to pull the wire tight around the hook. Be careful not to pull on that embedded hook too forcefully. You can help the wrapped wire 'grab' by squeezing it and the hook with pliers.

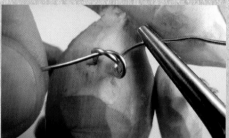

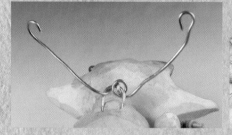

Now bend the ends of the wires over, and we're ready to add the flittery paper wings. Take one paper and add a thin layer of all-purpose craft glue to the bottom center.

Wrap the paper, glue side in, around one of the wires. Gather the paper tightly around the wire. The glue will help the paper grab itself as well as secure the paper to the wire.

I suggest wrapping a bit of ribbon in a crisscross around the gluey paper for extra security as well as a bit of prettiness. Obviously, tie the ribbon in a little knot and snip off the excess.

Repeat for the other wing.

Finally, slip a ribbon through the hook, tie the ends together and hang up your fabulous Flying Faerie Fox!

Friends of the Fox Faerie

Skunkarina

You can make all kinds of other faeries too! Here is a fragrant little skunk faerie with smaller ears than the fox and no foxy cheek poufs. She has a little bead cap for a crown, embedded with a headpin, and her wand is also a headpin with a bead at the tip and wire wrapped all the way down, to hold the bead in place.

Barry Beary Bearbear

You can make a little carved figure without wings. For this bear, I rounded the ears and made a little T-shaped nose. I also carved out paw-finger shapes on all his limbs. Don't forget to paint on his little pink footpads! (Log stool optional.)

The Hedgeblob

You don't even have to make your critter with articulated limbs to get that hand-carved folk art look. This little hedgeblob has two front paws and a perky mouse-like nose.

Moose are pretty amazing-looking creatures – they seem almost prehistoric, don't they? Those antlers are something a triceratops would be envious of. Of course, those antlers are a bit of a problem when creating a moose head bead. If we create the antlers realistically, they would stick out pretty far, and you could poke somebody's eye out. So, let's copy the Egyptian trick and just sorta' turn and flatten the perspective – still moosey, but not pokey!

special stuff you'll need

• beads, assorted sizes (I used disc-shaped shell beads, and pearls)
• headpins
• one 4mm dark, round bead (eye)
• mica powder: Brown

Are you ready to moose it up? Me too! Condition and mix up the moose clay blend (about half a package of each color is more than enough). Condition half a package of ecru for the antlers too.

clay colors
moose = golden brown
gold + burnt umber

2. antlers = ecru

Roll some of the moose clay into a ball – about as big as a chocolate truffle (mmmmm, that's sounds good right now... I'll be back in a minute....)

Form the ball into a log that tapers at one end. The thinner end will be his snout end, so don't make it too small (moosesesses have big nosesesses).

Bend the log over your finger into an arch.

Use a tool to make a crease that separates the head part from the rest of the neck part. This should make the bend less noodley and more angular. Make the head part so it is a little shorter than the neck part.

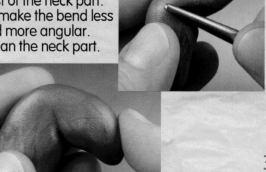

Press the end of the nose down a little so that the snout droops. There, that's more moosey already.

Now let's shape the other end. The head is in the classic "bust" style that cuts off at the lower neck. To make that more artistically pleasing (and less like a guillotine mishap), just use your fingers to gently pinch and pull the front part (the part under the face) into a bit of an angled point.

Good. Let's build up the face in the place where the eye will be. Roll out a small ball of clay (small pea size) and press it onto the face (just in front of the neck crease). Use a tool to smooth it into the face. It's ok to leave some tool streaks, as long as they look like fur texture.

Wire up a round bead in the usual way (check the back of the book for a refresher if you have short-term memory issues). Press it into the center of the mound we just added. Embed the bead into the clay deep enough so that no wire shows, if you can.

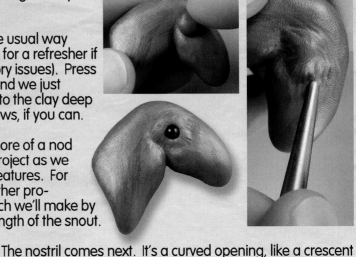

We're going to have a bit more of a nod towards realism with this project as we make more of the moose features. For example, moose have a rather pronounced facial groove, which we'll make by pressing a tool down the length of the snout.

The nostril comes next. It's a curved opening, like a crescent moon. Use a tool to press in an opening (I used the end of my GHI tool, it's shaped just right). The nostril is slanted parallel to the lines of the face.

Ok, enough realism – back to whimsy! How about a smile on the ol' moose? A happy moose is better than a grumpy moose. Use a needle tool to impress a line across the snout. Press it in at the bottom so he keeps a good bit of upper lip (moose have a lot of upper lip). The line should go all the way around to the front, but not too far unless he's a little nutz.

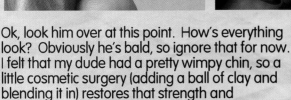

Now seems like as good a time as any to create a bit of definition around the nostril. Just a little pressing around the nostril will do it – not too deep.

Ok, look him over at this point. How's everything look? Obviously he's bald, so ignore that for now. I felt that my dude had a pretty wimpy chin, so a little cosmetic surgery (adding a ball of clay and blending it in) restores that strength and chin-liness so important to a young moose.

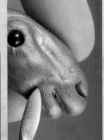

Pull that upper lip down a little – it's a moose thing.

If you go look at a moose (from a safe distance, of course), you'll notice some weird dangle thingy… no not there - under his face towards the neck. To add this distinctively moosey appendage, roll out a teardrop of clay, slice off the tip, press it onto the underside of his face and blend it in with a tool.

So far so good!

Next let's make the ear. You'll only need one, antlers hide the other side. Roll out a ball of clay (about the size of a chickpea).

Roll the ball into a teardrop. Now pinch and roll the fat end of the teardrop to make a little stem.

Use a tool to smoosh an indentation into the non-stem part of the clay shape.

Now hold it up so that the stem is facing forward (towards the right as you look at it) so that you can gently press the lower end of the ear to flatten it a little.

With your cutting blade, slice off the tip of the stem at an angle so that when you lay the ear against the head, it will angle nicely – not too flat and not too sticking-out.

Place the ear on the head to get an idea of how it will look. Adjust the angle of the cut if needed. Take it off and set it aside for now.

Time to make the antlers! Yay! Roll out a ball of the ecru clay (about the size of a small grape, it's ok if it's a red grape size this time).

Roll the ball into a teardrop. Do the stem thing again. Flatten the whole shape with your fingers to a little less than a quarter inch thick.

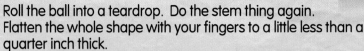

To add all the little points of the antler, just roll out a bunch of small, thin teardrops and press them onto the flattened shape.

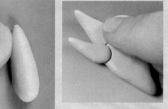

Start on the left side of the antler with several points in a row, then a bit of a gap, then a couple more, then one down at the bottom of the right side. (It's just a suggestion.)

Flip over the antler so far, and hold it in your palm so you can blend the clays together on the back side first.

Now blend the front side. Add additional stroke lines to give the whole antler texture. All the strokes should run down towards the stem of the antler.

Since the antler is big, and it will connect to the head at a rather small point, we'll need to add support to hold it all together. Snip off a piece of 20 gauge wire long enough to go though the center of the antler and still leave some wire to press into the head. Bend a hook in one end of the wire, then push the other end into the antler.

Use pliers to push the antler wire into the top of the moose head so that the antler clay touches the head clay.

Add a small snake of moose-color clay around the base of the antler to help connect them together. Blend it into the head side, but not the antler side.

Now we can press the ear into position and blend the clays together.

To give a sense of perspective, you may want to add the hint of a second antler behind this one. You can just make a partial antler – just a bit of base and the points that would show on the right side – and press it into place on the backside of the main antler.

Then I used a little wad of toilet paper to hold the top antler up a little, just because I felt like it. You can too, if you feel like it.

If you want your creation to be a chocolate moose, just add a dollop of whip cream.

Let's add more texture to the antlers. Little dimples with the rounded tip of a tool work really well.

Dots nice, ain't it?

More texture all around – strokes in the ears, furry lines in the face and neck. But leave the nose and lip smooth, ok.

At this point, you can be finished, just add a touch of powder and a hole for hanging and off to the oven. So skip over this next part if you like the un-adorned moose look!

For those of you still around, here's where it goes from a just a lovely moose head to more of an art piece. Adding embellishments is the way we make our creations personal and unique. I added shell disc beads because moose are North American forest creatures, and the natives of the northern woods often used shell discs to adorn their art. Also I just happened to have bought a stash of these really nifty vintage shell beads and I really wanted to use them in something.

Use any beads you personally find interesting. Add them with wire or headpin (that info is in the back, of course). Press the beads into place wherever you like. I started with a line up the length of the antler and then branched out.

Additional accent beads in his neck look good too. (And I couldn't resist one on his forehead, too.)

A touch of powders - russet to redden up his nose, gold to accentuate his eyes, and brown to darken the antler tips – and you're done!

Well, almost. Use a needle tool to pierce a hole through the moose where you will want the stringing wire to go later – usually through the forehead and out the back of the neck behind the ear works well.

Bake for the usual time and temperature. Add any bits of toilet paper to prop the antlers, if needed. Once he's baked and cool, add a patina of dark brown acrylic paint and a clear, protective coating, if you like.

Isn't he mooserific?

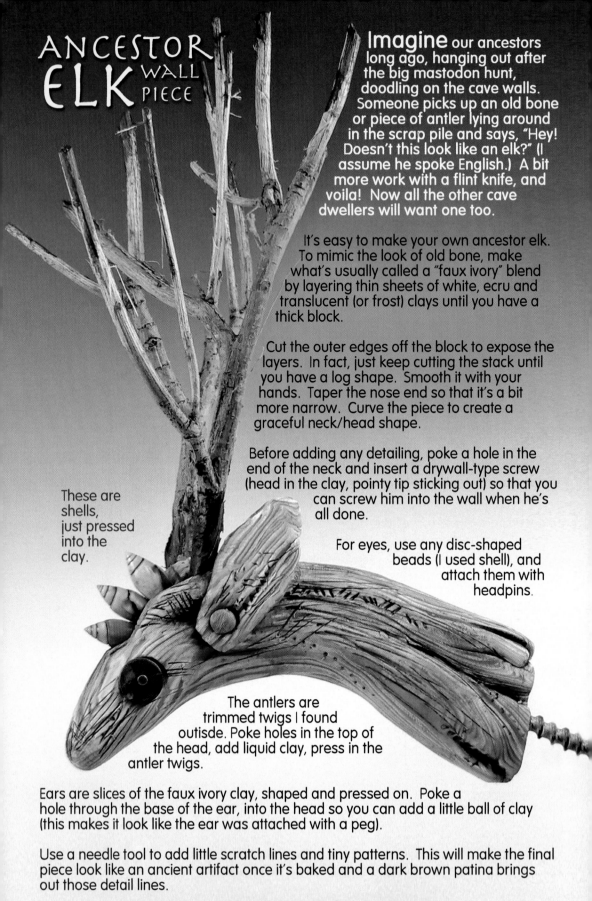

ANCESTOR ELK WALL PIECE

Imagine our ancestors long ago, hanging out after the big mastodon hunt, doodling on the cave walls. Someone picks up an old bone or piece of antler lying around in the scrap pile and says, "Hey! Doesn't this look like an elk?" (I assume he spoke English.) A bit more work with a flint knife, and voila! Now all the other cave dwellers will want one too.

It's easy to make your own ancestor elk. To mimic the look of old bone, make what's usually called a "faux ivory" blend by layering thin sheets of white, ecru and translucent (or frost) clays until you have a thick block.

Cut the outer edges off the block to expose the layers. In fact, just keep cutting the stack until you have a log shape. Smooth it with your hands. Taper the nose end so that it's a bit more narrow. Curve the piece to create a graceful neck/head shape.

Before adding any detailing, poke a hole in the end of the neck and insert a drywall-type screw (head in the clay, pointy tip sticking out) so that you can screw him into the wall when he's all done.

For eyes, use any disc-shaped beads (I used shell), and attach them with headpins.

These are shells, just pressed into the clay.

The antlers are trimmed twigs I found outisde. Poke holes in the top of the head, add liquid clay, press in the antler twigs.

Ears are slices of the faux ivory clay, shaped and pressed on. Poke a hole through the base of the ear, into the head so you can add a little ball of clay (this makes it look like the ear was attached with a peg).

Use a needle tool to add little scratch lines and tiny patterns. This will make the final piece look like an ancient artifact once it's baked and a dark brown patina brings out those detail lines.

And he's done! Screw him into the wall of your cave--the perfect spot to drape your bag after a long day of hunting and gathering!

One of the truly wonderful things about polymer clay as an art medium is that it can be so versatile – mimicking the appearance of plastic, leather, metal, wood, stone, ivory…. It can be contemporary, folksy, ethnic, ancient or antique. In this project we're going for an antique, metal look.

You can use the technique in this project to make any small, simplified shape look like an antique silver knickknack. I chose a rabbit because then I could title this project "Silver Hare" and get in a little play on words – it was a stretch, but I stand by my decision.

Condition some silver clay and rollout a small ball, about the size of a green grape (no, not a red grape or a purple grape, a green one!). Form it into an oval.

Press it onto your work surface to flatten the bottom. Press gently so that you don't flatten anything else other than the underside.

Roll out a small ball of clay (about the size of a baby pea) and press it onto one end (that's the butt-end now).

Roll out a larger ball (about the size of a peanut), form it into an oval, and press it onto the other end (that's the head-end now).

Use a tool to smooth the joins of head-to-body and tail-to-body. Be gentle and don't overdo it, it's especially important to keep the head looking distinct from the body.

special stuff you'll need
• silver leaf (substitute: silver-colored metal leaf) check the 'resources' section in the back of the book on where to get real silver leaf – it's worth it for this project!

• mica powder: silver

Since the ears need to stick up, adding a wire to support them is necessary. Snip about an inch of 20 gauge wire and press it into a flattened tiny blob of clay (about the same size as we made the tail ball).

Fold the clay around the wire and reshape the clay and then flatten it slightly (not too much or the wire will poke out!). Leave a little wire sticking out - it should look like a rice-sicle,

clay colors

silver = silver (duh!)

I got the inspiration for this project from my pal **Christi Anderson** (www.ElementalAdornments.com). She created this fabulous tiny rabbit out of fine silver and as soon as I saw it, I told her I was going to keep it AND create a project similar to it for polymer clayers. Luckily she let me get away with both! The rabbit in my project is less sophisticated than hers, giving it a bit more whimsical look. If you prefer the more artsy version, make the head and nose smaller.

39

Make the second ear in the same way.

With a tool, press a shallow indentation longways on the side of each ear.

Use needle-nose tweezers to press the ear wire into the top of the bunny's head. The indentation side faces outwards. Push the wire in as far as you can – ideally the clay of the ear will press in to the clay of the head. Use a tool to gently smooth the two together. You can add a tiny bit of additional clay if there are any thin spots.

The eye is very simplified. With a tool, press an indentation into the middle of the face on both sides (try to make sure they are even!) Next roll a teensy weensy ball of clay and press it gently into the indentation. It's best if not all of the indentation is filled by the ball.

To make the nose, roll out another little ball of clay and press it onto the tip of the snout. Flatten it a bit and then use a tool to smooth the top end only (the side facing the ears) onto the face.

Small ovals of clay pressed onto his underside in the appropriate feet areas make his paws. You can blend them in a little, or not.

Look him all over. Fix any problem areas, add a few slight indentations here and there to hint at furriness.

Next we're going to add the metal leaf. Using real silver leaf is much easier than using the silver-colored metal foils, but either will work. The real leaf is very, very thin, so it sticks to everything easily. It also likes to wander away, so make sure there's no drafts or breezes where you are working!

With tweezers, pull off a small piece at a time (a chunk of about an inch or more) and lay it directly onto the clay. Use a soft paintbrush to gently push the leaf down onto

the clay and wedge it into the crevices and angles. At this point don't worry if there are any gaps. Keep adding pieces of leaf and brushing them down. Don't forget the underside.

Once all the big areas are covered, you can grab smaller bits of silver and add them to the gaps. Leaf can overlap leaf, you'll be able to brush away anything that doesn't stick. Cover as much as possible. You'll need extra attention around the eye detailing and between the ears.

Finally, when you feel you can't add any more leaf, use silver-colored mica powder to dust the entire piece. This will help fill in all the small gaps.

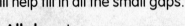

All done!

You'll notice little cracks all around (that's what makes him look antique!) Otherwise we could have just covered him entirely with silver powder or with a metallic silver coating (like guilders paste) once he was baked. The silver leaf crackles naturally as it is applied which is unlike any other metallic treatment we could have used. Nifty, huh?

Hey, have we used stamps in any of these projects? Not yet? Oh good! Then this will be a new taste treat! One of the things that polymer clay is reallllllly good at is being stamped with textures and designs. And of course, there are all kinds of things you can do with the clay once you've stamped it – you'll see....

These projects are going to be especially fun for me because this is the first time I've gotten to play with stamps that feature my own designs! Dynasty Stamps creates a wonderful line of stamps/texture sheets and I'm pretty jazzed to be one of the designers in their new "Artisan Series". (Check out the Resources at the end of the book if you're interested in more info.)

This leaping deer is one of several designs on my sheet. Look at all the things we can do with it!

Stuff you should know about using stamps with polymer:

. It's best to use a release agent on the stamp to help the rubber peel off the clay cleanly. You can use water or a powder (mica powder, baby powder or cornstarch). I prefer water.
. When you press the stamp onto the clay, try to use a firm pressure all around, don't rock the stamp or you'll get a double image. I find it helpful to hold the stamp in place with one hand while I push down with the other. For less distortion, pull the stamp away from the clay, not the clay away from the stamp
. And finally, once you're done, clean your stamp. There are components of the clay that can break down the stamps and shorten their usefulness - then you'd have to buy more, (which of course I'm totally fine with if they're my stamps, hee hee, but you may prefer not to have to). You can use water, or alcohol-free baby wipes to clean the stamps.

For these project techniques, you don't have to use my deer stamp, you can substitute any stamp you prefer. Once you've created each piece, it can be made into a brooch, wall piece or focal bead by adding the appropriate hardware (info for those tricks in the back, of course).

Let's start with the **"Rainbow Bright"** technique. Roll any light-colored clay through the widest setting on the pasta machine and press in the stamp design.

41

Use mica powders to liberally dust inside the lines of the design. I used brown in the deer lines, green in the grass and tree lines and blue for the circle border line. Don't worry about the mess.

Get a large piece of clear tape and lay it over the whole design (you can use the narrower scotch tape if you want, it just takes longer). Rub the tape down.

Peel the tape off! It will take the surface powder with it and leave the powder just in the lines of the stamp. You may need to repeat the process with several new pieces of tape in order to get all the surface powder off.

Use a craft knife to cut all around the stamp design. Bake. Seal with a clear coating.

Next is the "Swiss Chalet" technique - it's really two tricks in one – first mica powders (applied in a different way), and lots of vintage embellishments. Sound fun?

Start with a light-colored clay. Roll out a ball and flatten it with your fingers so that you have a flat clay "cookie" that will exactly cover the stamp area. Press it onto the stamp, then carefully peel them apart.

Add mica powders, but this time let's dust the surface of the clay design – green powder in the grasses and treetops, blue in the sky, brown in the tree trunks and branches, gold and brown in the deer body.

Bake the piece just like it is – the usual temperature, but for only about 20 minutes. Once it's cool, use a dark brown acrylic paint to antique it – this will fill all the outlines in with color.

Now to embellish it in hunting-chalet style. Look for ones that are branches and or leaves. Vintage-looking accents will work beautifully. To add them, we'll need a base of new clay to press the wires into, so roll out another sheet of clay (same color). Add some liquid clay to the back of the baked deer disc, and press it onto the sheet of new clay. Use a blade to cut the base clay, leaving about a quarter of an inch all around. Now add the vintage pieces in the usual way.

Bake again for the full time. Add more patina to the new area. Seal with a clear coating. (You should wear this one on your lederhosen.)

This next technique is the "Greenery Wreath" look. Make a pale-green clay blend. Press the stamp into the clay, and then cut it out around the border.

Wad up the clay scraps and roll them out into a sheet again. Use liquid clay to attach the deer disc to the new clay. Cut the new clay, leaving a quarter inch border.

For the next part I used these little molds of leaves that I made. You can use the same molds (info in the back of the book, of course), or make your own leaves and create molds from them, or make each leaf one at a time. It's all good!

To use the mold, press a little ball of clay into the mold, and pull it out. Press it onto the border.

Keep going all around the ring! You can use all the same leaf, or mix it up. You can also add little balls of clay as berries, and little wiggly snakes of clay as tendrils. Bake. Add patina. Classy, isn't it?

Now let's make the **"Molten Spike Medallion"**. This is the kind of piece you'd wear with your cape when you go out to battle werewolves, or listen to an opera.

Roll out some black clay, press in the stamp. Cut it out, but leave a thin border.

We're going to add some silver mica powder just to the surface of the design. Don't use a brush for this, because it's hard to keep the powder on just the surface. But if you get some powder on your finger and swipe it across the clay, you'll get the right effect.

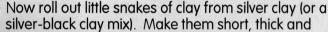

Now roll out little snakes of clay from silver clay (or a silver-black clay mix). Make them short, thick and pointy at both ends. Bend, curl and pinch them into molten spikes (you know what those look like, right?). Press them all around the medallion.

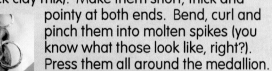

Some metal embellishments will add to the overall strength of the look, so add some! I used links from an antique-silver colored chain. Press them into the clay spike ring.

Dust silver mica powder to the tips of the spikes. Bake as usual. Now cape up, and head into the night with your deer of distinction!

There's one other technique,"Russian Night". Hmmm, I could show you how to do that… it's paint and resin and gold leaf pen and stuff… not really enough room left in the book to do it right…ok, so instead just go to my website and I'll show ya how to over there! It's like getting a little more book for free!

Here are **a few more techniques** for you to play with when creating with polymer and rubber stamps. (I used a few more designs from my "Capricious Creatures & Fab Foliage" stamp sheet, just because I can.)

This rustic wall piece is made by running some clays through the pasta machine, keeping the edges rough. Stack two sheets for a layered look. Press a design into the clay. You can make little accent stampings by rolling out a ball of clay, flattening it a bit, and pressing it into just one part of the stamp (for example, a leaf, and a curl).

This next piece uses the same technique (pressing the stamp into a rough sheet of clay). I used the faux ivory clay blend (remember from the elk page?). Press the stamp into the ivory clay. Bake and patina. This piece really comes together when you add the accents - waxed linen thread, driftwood, electroplated leaves and pebble beads. Delightfully primal, don't you think?

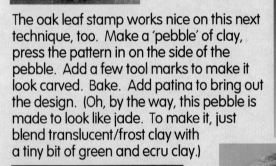

The oak leaf stamp works nice on this next technique, too. Make a 'pebble' of clay, press the pattern in on the side of the pebble. Add a few tool marks to make it look carved. Bake. Add patina to bring out the design. (Oh, by the way, this pebble is made to look like jade. To make it, just blend translucent/frost clay with a tiny bit of green and ecru clay.)

Ok, room for just one more technique. This is very easy, you've already done it with the Silver Hare project. Simply stamp a design into gold clay, cut around the border, then cover it with metal leaf (I used 23k. gold leaf). Bake. Add a little brown patina to fill in the outlines.

Hey, guess what? That's the end of all the projects. Did you like 'em?

Hey! I'm a woodland creature and I'M not in this book!!

Neener neener neener! I was on the very first page!

Hey! I thought making a dragonfly was supposed to be one of the projects in this book? Well, I guess since there was a dragonfly in the "Steampunkery" book, that would be kinda redundant. I'm prettier though, don'tcha think?

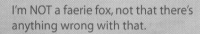

I'm NOT a faerie fox, not that there's anything wrong with that.

This wall piece is an online class, just in case you were wondering.

I'm shy.

Dragons live in the woods sometimes, who says they don't?

Me too! But I'm in "Steam-punkery"

I'm a woodland creature, but I'm **already** a project in the "Polymer Clay & Mixed Media" book

45

Polymer clay is fabulous stuff. Here are a few things you ought to know about using it:

You should **condition** clay before using – simply roll, fold, twist and smoosh until it is soft and pliable (or for faster results, use a pasta machine to roll the clay through, fold and roll again until soft). As clay ages, it may lose some flexibility, but there are several products available to add softness, such as Translucent Liquid Sculpey (also known as liquid clay). I also like using Sculpey Mold Maker clay (less messy).

All polymer clay is good, but I use and recommend **Premo brand** clay for the projects in this book. It's a perfect clay for sculpting.

Make special **blends** by mixing clay colors together. Press one or more colors together and run them through your pasta machine, then rip, stack and re-run multiple times. You can stop while there are still color variations visible, or you can keep mixing until the new color is completely blended.

When you aren't using it, you can **store** polymer clay in glass jars or in most brands of plastic zippered bags, or wrap it in plastic wrap. Store it out of direct sun, in a cool place for optimal awesomeness.

Clean your hands when switching from one color clay to another. If there is residue of color on them you'll get smudges (especially if you go from an intense color to white! Eek!) Wet wipes work well to clean your hands of clay residue, as does any soap with grit in it. Polymer clay does not thin with water.

Add **embellishments** like beads, metal, fibers and other mixed media to your clay while you are sculpting, then baked in place. Only things that would melt in the oven (like plastic) should be avoided. When in doubt, test bake a sample item.

Whenever possible, **anchor** embellishments into the clay with a headpin or wire 'tail'.

To add a wire tail: snip about an inch of 28 gauge wire; slip on a bead; pull the wire ends together; grip wire with pliers and twirl bead with fingers until it twists up to the bead; snip off the excess wire to leave about a quarter of an inch; bend the tip of the wire into a hook.

To use a **headpin**: slip on the bead; use wire cutters to snip off any excess wire to leave only about a quarter of an inch of wire; with pliers bend a hook into the end; press the bead (wire hook first) into the clay.

Sometimes you'll want to add a **pin back** to your piece to make a brooch. Bake your

piece for the full time and temperature; let it cool; add a bit of liquid clay onto the back of your piece where you want to attach the pin; lay the opened back of a hinged straight pin in the liquid clay; cover the pin back and liquid clay with a thin piece of fresh clay; bake again for 20-25 minutes.

Sometimes you'll want to add a **wire hanger** to your piece to make a wall piece. Snip a one inch piece of 20 gauge wire; bend it in half; use pliers to bend hooks in each end; set the hanger on the back of your baked piece; add a bloop of liquid clay on each hook end; cover the hook ends and liquid clay with a thin piece of fresh clay; bake again for 20-25 minutes.

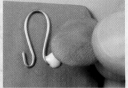

And finally, **baking your clay** -- the most important part of any project! Even the best creation in the world is trash if it melts and burns during baking! For these projects the "usual time and temperature" to bake Premo brand clay is at 275°F (130°C) for 45 minutes. The thicker the clay, the longer the time (I usually bake for 45 min. to an hour). For other brands, read their instructions (but it's usually very similar).

275° F for 45 minutes

Always preheat your oven - use an oven thermometer to keep an eye on the correct interior temperature. Polymer clay shouldn't be baked any less than 5° below than the recommended temperature, and not more than 10° above it. Too cool or for too short a time and the clay won't cure properly: too hot or for too long and the clay will scorch or even burn/melt entirely – icky!

Use proper **ventilation** when baking clay - some people are sensitive to the fumes. Any oven is fine – the farther from the heating elements your piece is, the less likely it will be to scorch from the spikes of the heating cycles. If you use a home oven, you can minimize polymer residue remaining behind by baking in a covered casserole dish, or inside an oven roasting bag (roll it and secure the open end). If you use a pan/dish/bag in baking your clay, don't later use it with food, duh.

You can bake and **re-bake** polymer multiple times – this is an awesome property of the clay! It allows you to firm areas as you go along. Use liquid clay on the baked clay to allow fresh clay to attach. The final baking time is always the full amount, no matter how many times you've already baked the piece.

Cured clay is very **durable, colorfast, lightweight** and **waterproof**. Thin pieces of clay are naturally very flexible.

If you like, you can add a **patina** to the clay once it is baked. To do this, brush acrylic paint onto the clay, a little at a time. Get it into all the cracks and crevices (don't worry if it gets on the embellishments). Immediately wipe it off the surface with very-wrung-out damp sponges (use several so you don't smear the paint all over). This will leave an antique-ing style coloring in the details only. Very nifty, I think.

When the paint is dry, you can brush on a **clear coating/varnish** to protect the piece. For these projects, you'll want to use a very low-gloss shine, so look for a matte or satin finish. I have several products that I use, especially the Studio Sculpey Satin Glaze (check my website store for the latest information since products change name and consistency – I'll keep ya up-to-date on the good stuff!) Just use a brush to apply to the baked clay, avoid getting any on the embellishments.

That's it! There's always lots more you can learn, but this is everything you need. Happy claying!

RESOURCES
Check these places out for some of the things used in the projects in this book (and just for fun stuff in general!)

www.**FireMountainGems**.com - beads, tools, wire, jewelry supplies

www.**CkoopBeads**.com - enamel headpins and other enamel accents

www.**WhimBeads**.com - beads, findings

www.**SpecialtyBeads**.com - ribbons, findings

www.**PolymerClayExpress**.com - clay supplies

www.**ClayFactory**.net - clay supplies, mica powders

www.**MisterArt**.com - craft supplies, paper

www.**KabelaDesign**.com - reproduction vintage pieces

www.**FiligreeandMore**.com - wholesale vintage pieces

www.**RioGrande**.com - jewelry findings, stamp/texture sheets

www.**CreativeWholesale**.com - wholesale clay supplies, craft andjewelry supplies

www.**NightSideStudios**.com - this is my 'eye guy' – check out his other fun stuff!

www.**CForiginals**.com - I've tried to carry lots of the items you'll need for my projects on my site. You'll find the special designer stamps used in this book, as well as "squirrel tail" wool, lampwork eyes, mica powder, silver leaf, resin, mini molds & mold making materials, vintage and enamel goodies, clay supplies, pin backs, and of course my favorite tools!

WANT MORE CLAY FUN?
http://groups.yahoo.com/group/cforiginals
is my chat group where the nicest group of polymer enthusiasts swap stories, accomplishments and encouragement – join us!

other titles by christi friesen

the CF Sculpture series:

Book 1. Dragons
Book 2. Welcome to the Jungle
Book 3. Under the Sea
Book 4. Cats Big & Small
Book 5. Down Under
Book 6. Birds of a Feather

Steampunkery

Polymer Clay
and Mixed Media:
  together at last

Coming Next...
in the CF sculpture series

book **8**

Dogs